In the Arms of Words

Poems for Disaster Relief

All profits from this book go to AmeriCare. www.americares.org

In the Arms of Words

Poems for Disaster Relief

edited by Amy Ouzoonian

Foreword by Fatima Shahnaz, Ph.D.
Preface by Robert D. Wilson

Sherman Asher Publishing

Book Design & Layout By Scott Emmer

Sherman Asher Publishing
P.O. Box 31725
Santa Fe, NM 87594-172
www.shermanasher.com

The poems below have been published in the respective publications listed with them. The authors have given permission to reprint them in this anthology.

"An Argument With Memory" by Marge Piercy, *Prairie Schooner*, Spring, 2002.
"Basket of Figs" by Ellen Bass, *Mules of Love* (BOA Ed. LTD., 2002).
"Clear White Stream" by Marilyn Chin, *The Phoenix Gone, The Terrace Empty*.
"Come Here. Take Heart" by Verandah Porche, *Third Page*.
"Curve" by R.M. Engelhardt, *Georgetown Review*.
"Gathering the North Wind" by Patricia Wellingham-Jones, *Manzanita Quarterly*, 2001.
"Pain Is God's Love" by Maria Alexander, *Biting Midnight: A Feast of Darksome Verse*, by Maria Alexander and Christina Kiplinger-Johns (Medium Rare Books, 2002).
"Shoulders" by Naomi Shihab Nye, *Red Suitcase* (BOA Ed. LTD, 1994).
"Spring" by David Oliveira, *Art/Life*, 1996.
"The Moon Will Claim Me" by Diane di Prima, *Long Shot* #22.
"The Orphans of Tangshan" by Colette Inez, *Family Life*, Story Line Press.
"These Bones Remember" by Anthony Russell White, *Clackamas Literary Review* V:1, Spring/Summer, 2001.
"The Stream" by Dale Edmands, nominated poem of the month for May 2003 in the IBPC,. (InterBoard Poetry Competition). http://poetry.about.com/library/bl0503ibpcentries.ht-ml.
"Upside Down River" by Tad Wojnicki, *Simply Haiku* Jan.-Feb. 2004.
"Walking Through Fallen Berries" by Tara L. Masih, *Red River Review*, Aug. 2001.
"White Diamonds" by Prasenjit Maiti, *River Babble*, issue 3. http://ice-flow.com/riverbabble/issue3/whitediamond-s.html.
"You See How It Happened" by Laura Foley, *Guidance for Body Mind and Spirit*, Care2.com.

In Loving Memory Of
Professor James Lynch

Table of Contents

Foreword

This anthology, in memoriam for the victims of the tsunami, is a labor of love, an epiphany that reflects the congruent tributes of some of the most gifted trans-continental poets of our time. The message behind this selfless homage to the dead is, indeed, a serendipitous moment; it confirms our shared humanism, taps our sense of vulnerability, the fragility of mortal life transcending thousands of miles of separateness.

We continue to hear their voices from water, shifting tides and trade-winds that sensitize our awareness to the transience of our consumer societies, the mundane narcissistic trivia that divert us from our innate humane-ness. Death, the great equalizer, strikes indiscriminately of race, caste, class or creed. At this final reckoning, the universality of bereavement forces us to introspect, to salvage shipwrecked lives and rehabilitate scarred orphans, the children who were the majority of the casualties. This anthology personalizes a closure for survivors and eye-witnesses across the world while also touching the core themes that pulled together so many sensitive souls. These poems extol the martyrdom of those whose horrific wanton deaths have instilled an awareness within us dissolving geographic boundaries, and are a metaphysical affirmation of our universal human condition.

Stylistically, the shockwaves of the tsunami have also had a seismic effect by radicalizing a new vision in post-modernist poetry. The trauma of "thanatosis," death, has galvanized a new consciousness diverging from the abstract intellectualism or existential nihilism of the last millennium. This paradigm-shift from the "meism" of Western cultures focuses on the ground realities of the Third World such as the eradication of poverty, starvation, dislocation, displacement, the gypsy-races and refugees, the deprivation of adequate amenities—water, shelter, employment. This dystopic worldview reflects multiculturalism in mixed metaphors and imagery that collate the paradoxes of the mundane; revitalizing conventional poetic axioms of new blood transfused. The stylistic versatility ranges from the inspirational to the elegiac tradition; poets memorialize the dead, cope with loss and grief, pathos and bereavement. In *The Last Wave* Michael Hillmer introspects, "On their lips / empty eye sockets fill / with mud and skin / bursts open under wedding bands / extinct beings transfigure / into acts of love / beside the bodies of our species / we are made human again."

This consummate humaneness is the process of transformation unearthed by innumerable poets, from Thomas J. Baier's focus on visual minutiae, "The day opens like a snap pea / becomes a string of memory

pearls" to the finessed sensibility of Diane Ackerman. Citing *The Global Language Monitor* Jennifer Browne writes, "Disaster changes use of word tsunami." Other poets scope dehumanizing cultural myths in a world of alienation, plumbing the imminence of death as poignantly as Grecian Odes, or Miltonian pathos. In *Nam jai*, "Do you remember the trips we took / to the white sand beaches of Ilocos? That is how I chose / to remember you, my dear friend."

Without further revealing the myriad poems in this rainbow gathering of creative artists, I should like to voice a universal 'cri de Coeur' in *Kaira, Peace* (as sung by Papa Susso to Bob Holman): "Kaira is a word / It is the word for Peace ... Slavery abolished but people still fight for power ... With people dying in Iraq even though the war is not a war / Kaira, the word for Peace / Please Peace Now / Kaira is the word for Peace."

Hasn't the tsunami death-toll indelibly sent out the message, that the 'collateral damage' of epic Trojan wars entrenched in millennial hatreds makes this song of 'Kaira' resonate in our hearts and souls?

Please, Peace Now.

—*Fatima Shahnaz, Ph.D., Sorbonne University, Paris, France President, India Peace Organization International human rights activist*

Preface

"Tonight the full moon / is all flesh..." wrote, one of the contributors, Kate Gray, in her poem *Moon Over The Tsunami*. "...Touch it / and you touch / what the ocean / took from you."

It was a hot, humid morning on the 26th of December, 2004, in Aceh, Indonesia. The weather was typical for that part of the world. Fishermen readied their catch for the market-place, vendors laid out their wares on tables; the smell of hot bread, like a serpent, wove its way through village streets.

Without warning, an earthquake, measuring 9.2 on the Richter Scale, set into motion a tidal wave that would destroy this beautiful, sometimes controversial Islamic region. The effects would leave the lands' inhabitants in a state of shock, fear, sorrow, and economic uncertainty. In moments, a huge gray wave swept over the area, instantly killing thousands. The landscape was reminiscent of Hiroshima after the atom bomb had been dropped. I remember seeing newscasts in the Philippines, Indonesia's closest neighbor, my second home. I couldn't believe my eyes.

the sky
a gray porridge
stirred by trees

And that was just the beginning. Several countries, with coastlines facing the Indian Ocean, were also assaulted by the watery monster, making the tsunami one of the deadliest natural disasters in modern history.

the cries
of starving children,
not monkeys

The aftermath of this disaster sickened my stomach. Bridges and roads were demolished. Many of the victims were cut off from those who could supply them with aid. Only help from helicopters came, attempting to land on small makeshift landing pads. On the beaches, and in what once were villages, lay stacks of rotting bodies – their stench unbearable.

sandy beach
blowflies hover above
the dead

There was not enough water and food or the medicine and medical aid necessary to treat the injured. Untold thousands were without shelter, sanitary facilities, or electricity. Many children were orphaned. Some had been kidnapped by sex traders.

two weeks later
wave after wave
of bad dreams

Thousands more would die in the coming months and days from disease, starvation, and injury.

Poets are, by nature, intuitive and empathic. Poetry appeared, within minutes, in online forums and in print. Touching, poignant, stirring poems. Amy Ouzoonian took it upon herself to collect the best of these poems and place them in an anthology, with all profits going to the victims of the tsunami and now of the hurricane disaster.

Read these poems. They rouse, they linger, they place you in the sandals of those who were there. When you are finished, share this book with another. And another.

—**Robert D. Wilson,** *owner/managing editor, www.simplyhaiku.com*
Author of Vietnam Ruminations, www.vietnamruminations.com

Introduction

In the Arms of Words: Poems for Disaster Relief

Every morning, since 1995, I have tried to make a point to write while listening to the radio, sitting outside at a park, or after reading the newspaper. Someone once told me, writing is about listening to the world around you and translating those messages.

During the week that followed the tsunami that hit India, Thailand and surrounding countries, I was listening to NPR and soaking in the emotions, images and struggling voices traveling over radio waves. The media reports became poems, the poems became an idea, which, in the days to follow, became the conception of an anthology intended to raise funds for tsunami relief. This anthology would consist of poets writing poems that would not evoke or describe the devastation that survivors had to endure, but poems that evoked a sense of hope in the face of disaster.

One week after I posted a call for submissions on two or three message boards on the Internet, poems and inquiry letters poured in from Africa, India, Japan, France, Italy, Spain, Serbia, Norway, and all over the U.S. My inbox was packed with voices wanting to soothe, sympathize, and reach out to the survivors. These poets wanted to assure the victims, they are not alone and that help is on the way.

One poet, from Serbia, captured me the most. She sent me her poems with a cover letter explaining this was all she had to give the survivors and that she didn't have the extra monetary funds to donate, her poetry contributions were all she could give. The opportunity, to offer her hope and words to the victims, was a gift to her as well.

After hurricane Katrina left Mississippi and Louisiana in ruins, many contributors of this anthology asked me if I was going to do another anthology and though I wanted to do something to help, I knew it would be impossible to drop all the responsibility of this anthology, only to take on another project. However, I wanted to help the survivors and send aid to rebuild the city and the spirit of New Orleans.

So, I have decided to divide the proceeds raised from sales of the anthology to Katrina survivors and Tsunami survivors, and so as not to confuse people and to let everyone know that this book was not only intended for tsunami relief and that it is meant to target a sense of hope extracted out of any disaster, I changed the title to *In the Arms of Words: Poems for Disaster Relief.*

   I believe that this book was intended to bear that name and I'm glad that it has evolved into a book that provides healing as well as strength for people who've been through disasters, large-scale and minor, natural and man-made. This book is for survivors, held in the arms of words.

—Amy Ouzoonian, *Editor*

In the Arms of Words

Poems for Disaster Relief

Law of the Ocean

Karla Linn Merrifield

consider this afternoon
moments before the predicted
2:24 post-meridian high
two days before Winter Solstice:
the verticality of tides

do not say of them
that they come in
say they rise   they climb
to claim the tracks of animals
who live on this edge
the tracks of those
who would silently stalk
the strand

voici! here a cloven-hoofed deer
has passed through a pass
between shallow dunes into the marsh
voila! sand dollars hidden just below
the surface of this stretch of beach
breathing their rings of air

there sanderlings have skittered an array
of soft splinters with their tiny
tined feet   a winding whiplike
trail embossed in moistest sand?
Sign of the Atlantic Augur
auguring the necessity
of slow motions at this hour

in the time it takes
a sole bottle-nosed dolphin
to leap northward across
the eastern horizon
in so short or so long
a time, the tides will shift

they will fall
they will go down
with diving cormorants
in the sea   trackless
otherwise unseen

The Upside Down River

Tad Wojnicki

We sit where the Salinas River empties into Monterey Bay. Swept,
we're not. This late, hardly any of it shows.

river mouth grill
fried trout at the table
in the river bed

The river may not be showing, but it is gurgling underneath the sand
through the entire length of the Salinas Valley, soaking everything from
onions to oranges. Known as "The Upside Down River," it is the biggest
underground stream in America.

lovers long gone
sit by the river
teacher's mouth dry

January 1, 2005

What I have learned in 2004 is that,
should my pets unexpectedly
become agitated, should they scratch
at the door until I let them outside,
should they make a dash for high ground
as fast as their furry legs can run,
I will be scooping up my children
and getting us the hell out of Dodge.

Jörgen Johansson

treacherous sea
the bell buoy
dead silent

förrädiskt hav
klockbojen
dödstyst

Grace

Diane Ackerman

I

White carnations
slouch
in a green glass vase
before the picture window,

as pink tremolos
of sunset,
whole sentences of light,
drift through
the Venetian blinds.

The sun keens itself
in a curve
of the vase,
fizzing yellow.

II

On the lawn of memory,
    violets suddenly appear: each a sensation

like a note, but without the dirge of loss,
    translucent, welcome, unexpected.

Photo albums open their leaves
    with a calm that seems phenomenal.

Tonight the sun reclines in the sky,
    and time is a kneeling animal.

Spring

David Oliveira

I walk to the front of the house
carrying a single cup of water

to an iris planted weeks ago,
when spring was an acceptable risk,

a prayer offered with dirty fingers for
this first blossom unfolding all it has

into the familiar shadow of myself,
now silent before the gift of these

perfect petals, astonished that another
season comes around to its promise

just when loss seemed all that was sure,
all there could be after a cup

empties its small storm
over thirsty leaves and bare feet.

She Wrote

Lois P. Jones

Today you counted
handprints along the shoreline.
Families stack fronds,
burn empty boats to leave
no perishable remains.

daughter sees blemish

Ray Craig

daughter sees blemish
reported missing from Phuket, Thailand

tsunami ghost gasping for stray dogs
monk scrubs skin with cassette

anonymous tongue offering lamp and rice
feet stubbles in mud

**
women and children return from the river
and smoke sago leaves to warm their mouths

brambles thickly clog in luminous stray

Simatalu, Indonesia

Shin Yu Pai

240,000 lost to
flood & deforestation
can't see the forest for the trees

After the Wave, Another: Nam Jai*

literally, water of the heart, compassion   *Laurie Klein*

I remember the sloe-eyed children of Buriram.
Sleek bobs, white cotton blouses and navy skirts,
all that giggling—at first I couldn't tell you apart,
couldn't affix unsayable names to each face. I have
slow eyes. Impossible,
though, to overlook hairlines stippled with nits,
and, having weathered bouts of lice back home,
for so many weeks—forgive me—dreading
exposure, I held you with gaze alone

until the last. Midnight on New Year's Eve,
Anita labored in Yan Yao Temple, unloading
the limp bodies, unnamed, etched with wrack.
Swathed in white, workers wore masks.
Rubber-gloved in Zen's orange, they moved
quietly, like monks at their prayers,
contained, in contagious reverence.
And the bereft? "Nam jai," she said,
"without exception, kind, patient. Understanding." No, don't look

away from this; behold the temple, for some
see the body as passage, a dimming hall
between rooms, doors closed, opening;
others implore the man of sorrows. Tonight
I read about mourners of four faiths
keeping vigil, together releasing candles in paper
balloons, shapely, luminous as those faces I left behind
in the Land of Smiles, each lantern lifting off,
breasting the darkness.

So You Will Not Ask God Why

Chelle Miko

Remember the Johnstown flood
was not some gargantuan thirst of God,
but one too many raindrops
in a manmade dam. Forget the plan
women and *children* first. What are the odds
of a river sweeping them from behind
wooden words like *chair* and *bible* and *stair*?
What's the possibility that each one of two
thousand tongues bobs a prayer
against the pink roof of a mouth? Before their husbands
brothers or sons can stop a rooftop raft from sinking
with their voices. Forget the bodies
that lap the shore, hoisted by the wind
and rooted by windows, clocks, or doors
pinned in their bones. How full.
How full the river. Forget the fishers
of men. Who can blame them
for each pickpocket they catch
and lynch? One neck for every heirloom
pinched from the dead, one beating
heart for every picture scraped from a locket,
neatly as a clam from its shell,
and one shooting victim, a pauper who begs
for his breath, after pocketing a little girl's ring
finger, snipped from her cold hand.
Remember a bulrush ark with room enough
for one. How smoothly it was pushed back
into the wide womb of water. How full
the manger. How full the river. Can you
stand an answer? Before your lips try
to shape a question, remember the darkest current
has never held a drop of anger.

The Visible Ones "Eat Leaves*"

Barbara Tomaine

When love lives in two places,
mountains break,
breath comes inside out,
lungs exhale trees,
words rise
out of chairs,
waking is dying
every morning.
Forever is inside a wave
that walked dry tears away
into the bright, blue sun.

*Description of hunger as "eating leaves" taken from Reuters, Tsunami
Rescue Nurse, Linley York

Sensing Foreignness

Mary Strong Jackson

Sometimes the quiet becomes another country
and the only sure things
are the cross-hatched lines
where thumbs and forefingers connect
and the way the hand moves
free from thought.

22

ellipses in the carpet

James Warner

Pushing a shopping cart
            around a stairway
in the basement,

Sometimes I'm the stairway
and you're the shopping cart.

Sometimes you're the shopping cart
and I'm running late.

Usually we are both mules with hands—
No bridle
No rope
just pushes and circles.

We are never the room that holds us.

In dreams we long to be carried
out of orbit,
up the steps
            and into the lobby
            where days wait
            beyond doors.
But we wake to the motion
sickness of awkward circles
or the elevation of downward
slopes never moving
in any real direction,
just fulfilling scientific definitions:
slaves to Newton and each other.

Hollow Bones

Renee Roehl

There is something you should know:
when bones are hollow
flight becomes necessary.
Too much depends on
the brown and black wing. I've heard
all birds love red
just as all humans adore soaring
stars that sing
arias as they rocket
past whirling planets.

If only the clouds wept
blood instead of water
the consecration
of holy lands
would not involve bombs.

This is what you should know:
each bony finger indicating the wind's direction
has unhindered aim. It involves more
than a wish for absolution. Split open

the atoms of stains and tints:
color the midnight a pale silver.
When the stars pass
quietly through the scorched dark,
one sleeping civilian
        will dream
        of feathers

and all the birds will be safe.

What You Will Believe

Irene O'Garden

The orange you will believe in, and her love.
Your mother's fingers peel its shimmer skin,
spritzing citrus cross your nose, and in
your eye, so that you could not see—above

and then upon you—a single stinging tear
obscures what you will never now believe:
the whole upended ocean in a heave
drowning, drowning all you know. What you called here

is smashed to silt; what you called her
the gushing salt erased, but for that final taste,
that segment of sweet orange she passed—
her parting gift: distraction and the blur.

All we love becomes debris.
You. Me. Why fight the battering?
We're not made of matter, but of mattering,
Love answers, turns and tends catastrophe.

dinosaurs

Ameena Mayer

they came, grey, liquid dinosaurs
rolling in mammoth mouths
the vibrant colours of life into thick, wet balls,
spitting them back to sea.

strange, these collages of bloody limbs,
litter, disease, smeared grizzly
across screens: their uncanny resemblance to
images of dead Sudan villages, refugee camps   we
saw long ago.
the difference: the raucous clank of coins for
Asia from G8 governments,
so they can thrust
resorts like nails into soft, red wound

a bunch of hopeless refugees
who can't offer us much, they say;
besides, the world says, that crisis is as old as
prehistory, and we've no more interest in the
footprints of dinosaurs.

Stone

Lucy Anderton

"In a visit to Auschwitz,
Bush sets out to repair ties strained
       by Iraq War." —CNN, June 1, 2003

Perhaps.
Perhaps something
Has happened. Perhaps

The ashes
Descended, ringed

The man and woman posing
For Press, fingers just
Touching

Oven Doors,
Positioning a fresh cut

Rose
On the silenced
Iron.

Perhaps the bone hewn
Stones that sleep (but do not

Sleep) beneath
Those tracks cracked
Under his executive

Walk, the air with a grayed
Unfolding eye finally closed

Down his throat—the fugue
Of 6,000,000
Dead

Fell
Through his lung.

And if he saw
The words carved
In the night-

shelves: *"Ich bin,*
Ich bin!"— If

The sky began
To flatten
him.   Later,

In the hotel bed, he takes
Off his shoes, sees

The smooth round bone
Chip wedged in the dark
Sole, prizes it out—

It is there in his palm,
Whispering, *What*

Have you done? What
Have you
Done?

Swim

Natasa Bozic Grojic

He loves the sea.
It is his friend,
the brother I can't give him.
He has no fear.

"Swim," he says,
and never turns back.
"Swim," he says.
One of the few words he knows.
"Swim," he says
even when he goes to sleep.
"Swim tomorrow," he says.
"Swim," he said today.
I should never have let him go.
I should have come along.
I see him now.
"Swim," he says
and never turns back.
He is just a baby.
He can't find his way home.
and it is past his bedtime.

Plivam*

Voli more.
Ono je njegov drug,
 jedini koga ima.
Ulazi bez straha.
Ni da se osvrne.
"Plivam", kaze.
Zna samo nekoliko reci.
"Plivam", kaze
cak i kada podje na spavanje.
"Sutra plivam", kaze.
"Plivam", rekao je danas.
Nije trebalo da ga pustim.
Trebalo je i ja da podjem.
Kao da ga vidim.
Ulazi bez straha.
Ni da se osvrne.

Jos je mali.
Nece umeti sam da se vrati kuci
i trebalo bi da je odavno u krevetu.

Translation by author.

The Second, Vacation

Frank Simone

you're not a tourist anymore
and
there is never enough time,
before it is over,

the snapshots of where you have been
will never get developed,
remaining amidst the clutter of routine
traded in,

for that long awaited respite
you thought would never come
all of a sudden arrives
leaving a last minute decision
of what to take with you
and
what to leave behind
has to fit in one piece
of luggage

that one porter will carry
from the boat, to the lobby,
up to a room with a view
where you have never been before
but knew you would eventually be

lounging on a reclining chair
by the sea, under
the sun,
the waiter finally comes
dressed in white
as white as
the beach you're on
pours
a drink
and it spills all over you
"Sorry"
with one single gesture
a dark hand
wipes it all a way.

Shoulders

Naomi Shihab Nye

A man crosses the street in rain,
stepping gently, looking two times north and south,
because his son is asleep on his shoulder.

No car must splash him.
No car drive too near to his shadow.

This man carries the world's most sensitive cargo
but he's not marked.
Nowhere does his jacket say FRAGILE,
HANDLE WITH CARE.

His ear fills up with breathing.
He hears the hum of a boy's dream
deep inside him.

We're not going to be able
to live in this world
if we're not willing to do what he's doing
with one another.

The road will only be wide.
The rain will never stop falling.

On the Path to Jericho

Helen Losse

 I walk the path to Jericho—
plagued by uncertainty.

"Is the man wearing a top coat
my neighbor?" A girl nudges me,

startles me with gentleness. We dance.
And the way she tells the story:

No one dances alone. "Include
is a verb," she explains.

"Am I wearing the clothing of a liar?"
I ask. Thankfully, she does not answer me.

Andrew Riutta

pulled by water
to another dream...
the earth still in my pocket

"City of the Sea"

Title inspired by a poem by Walt Whitman   *Fatima Shahnaz*

the roaring sea at war
thrashing its octopus waves
belching its dogs
this burning ocean
this sea of blood
this apoplectic Biblical scourge of
the whale-jaw
vomiting anguished, meaningless lives snapped to
driftwood shipwrecks in the centrifugal savagery of
nature's 'shock and awe'

a tropical paradise
on a 'silk and saraband day'
a Delmore Schwartz poem
turned to beaches of desolation
shells of dismembered lives, severed torsos
a liquefied holocaust of barbed wire water foaming the
last eddying riptides of a Pan-Asian Atlantis
cities forever lost
in the sea's eternities

those splintered palm fronds enlaced with children's
fingers
who didn't want to let go of
futures unlived
my kinsmen walk beneath the waves
of nuke-black spillage
In the fathomless Beast's belly
dead men, women, infants morph
to algae, kelp, plankton, brine
their saline hair entwined in coral reefs on Phuket
Beach
anemones on the coromandal coasts
of Indian archipelagos
Tamil Nadu, Car Nicobar, the Andamans
Lost tribes in primal Circe's grotto
Sirens lure the shipwrecks to the oceanbed
Children buoyed like sea-drift, broken matchsticks in
the seething cauldron
Of the killer tsunami savaging
the Indian Ocean, Bay of Bengal
Bleached bones, bloated bodies washed ashore

disemboweled
With pearls for eyes
Swished in the wringer of the Great subequatorial
Laundromat

Swedish relatives scanning photographs looking beneath
the fetid blankets of putrefying flesh to salvage
rancid memories
Death, the great equalizer, grinds brown-and-white
races in mass-graves
the diminution of faceless Asians
Like swarms of diseased mosquitoes
Dwarfed by First World tourists in bathing-suits and
five-star hotels
Stripped ashen by
Death's imperialism

Father Sanders rides a skiff calling to Jesus walks
the waves to safe harbor
But where are the Hindu orphans of Sri Lanka, Tamil
Nadu
100,000 Muslims of Aceh
Hard to identify amidst bulldozers and mass funeral
pyres who was Episcopalian, Asian, Buddhist
or know the difference
'them' from 'us'

missionaries spread their fishing nets
the fishers of souls come to redeem displaced pagan
populations
Ahabs on the quest
To bring Moby Dick home
To Christendom
From paradise lost
Here only silent lambs
in a murderous sea,
lists of missing persons, bereaved families,
crocodiles scathed by nuked water beneath
the roar of death's
city of the sea.

Pain Is God's Love

Maria Alexander

Pain is God's love
He said
Legs folded lotus
On the bed
Of imported pillows
As he spoke to us
His spiritual students.

Pain is God's love
I said
As the needle
Slipped into my wrist
Into the nerve
And I called out his name
All the numbers and letters on
The license plate of his Mercedes
And the colors of his silk paintings
In the third-floor hallway.
He responded by telling me
I was too self-absorbed...

God-absorbed
And nag champa blind
My mind went white.
The nurse stroked my brow
As I shuddered.
You're doing very well,
The doctor said.
"I have a high pain threshold,"
I replied
Tears in my eyes
And I remembered
I have eighty dollars
Until the next disability check arrives.
And when the doctor left
The nurse and I talked
About karma and fate
How nothing's safe
And she said,
"Spiritual security
Is your only good bet."
I whispered,

"What a hard lesson that is."
And she cried.

Here in my bliss
In my handless
Nothingness
I say
Pain is God's love.
And I wish he knew
How much
God hated him.

Floater

Gary Lehmann

The image
of the doorknob
floats at the level of my bed
separating
and then superimposing itself
over again
as my eyes
adjust
slowly
to the morning light
without you.

Returning

Katherine James

It slipped beneath the men
like a soft earth-swallow,
the hull beneath them a spoon,
and the half alive fish, slippery
wafers of mercy.

If they had heard
somehow, the honest groanings
of the original pain— deep rearrangements
and matters unseen— the horizon would have
sucked like hope and laughed like hate,
a gray line of smoke transgressing
knowledge.

Now, at night they fear their own harbor,
and the fish, once their friends,
are dropped in the boat like prison nails
picked from the sea, elongated barbs
and metallic movement,
glistens of chain mail
covering nothing.

In darkness they wait
for color, for promise,
that the soggy mound of chewed up earth
might show itself like a slut,
curl a finger repeatedly in gestures of lust.

The fishermen move, powering forward.
They have nowhere else to go.

Walking Through Fallen Berries

Tara L. Masih

Plimouth Plantation, 1992

Distant daughter of Hobbamock,
paid to stand watch over remains
of his past life.
Hut, line, clay pots, baskets—Homesite—
rebuilt for us tourists,
pilgrim land now walked by the world.
I want to know how they survive today,
the Wampanoag's,
the rest,
in such hostile territory.
I have to break through character,
through script,
through recitations on clay
and corn
to get to this woman's
heart.
Her war mask slowly cracks
and opens
like a gift,
and I receive
her answer:
"Because we love the land."
How rich, to love so surely it carries you through the death of
tradition,
self,
soul—
or not . . .
And I imagine it is like walking
through fallen berries,
trying to shake free
the heavy, rotten deeds
of past and present
that cling to
a great spirit.

Leaving

David Chorlton

Some of us sink into our seats and finger
tickets as if they were rosaries,
and with a stale voice announcing departures
ringing in our ears
look down at the countries
we are leaving. Others simply disappear

and surface on the other side of a border
or an ocean. Some of us tossed a coin
and it came up foreign,
some held a compass
and walked where the trembling needle pointed.
Some of us had in-flight meals,
others drank water on the run,

and the rest never say how they survived the journey.
We are a statistic on the tables
that measure restlessness, one in thirty-five
of the world population
whose memories never match their surroundings.
Our maps have arrows instead of frontiers

to show how we move. You can see them
on those slide shows
that monitor unrest, the ones that are displayed
when the room is dark

and nobody knows who is sitting
in the seat beside them . . .

post-diluvian

Steve Dalachinsky

relax
            real light surrounds your eyes

   this is one way of ha(l)ving things
this is another
                        there is more than one way to skin a cloud
      pay a check
                        extinguish a fire

so the man with little to say distinguished himself again by saying too
much

stuck between tinsel & crumble
more than one way to extinguish a life
tie up the laces

it's not as if hands were unique
microphones tilted—
                        transforming grass into hardware
   into liguid
            tilt sign tilt sign

i stood somewhere beneath the tilt sign & then i cracked
stood for a moment   below my waist
                        & could
feel the plates shifting

bone dead & yet the flesh so much alive
rotted in spots
dodging again yet another wild pitch
earth laboring
final beams falling against discounted space
ruthless & wreckless
balance here
yet unaware / or uncaring
as your G/d might
be

i think i'm dying of cancer
she says i just have a bad cold

how does the death of 1000's

41

stack up against my problems?

earth laboring

coughs convulsively

nose runs one instant
stuffed up the next

back & ribs
cracking

my plates seem to be shifting
i am weighted in soft blue tissues
there is a rumbling in the street

i saw 3 cats as i precariously scuttled from one event to the next
the horizon never changing
nor the weather
only my temperature going from cold to hot
luckily they were all black & white

it is not about more bodies
or less
but about a contracting of space
an expanding
like a yawn
a fart
a belch

not about something in the present
but something from the past
that has changed the future

i spin within this axis

this is not a postcard
the sun re-emerging after a storm

shadows on a once cluttered
landscape
the sea itself again

the larger part

is always hidden beneath the surface
these are many different things
that are happening
even birds have deep memories
a germ of a melody
ruffled

                              i carried 15 notebooks
on
my shoulders today
                                   what was left of
38
yrs of writing
     (i lost a few yrs when the ground began to shift)
                                   then i put them
down

        as i walked calmly back to my room
           i encountered 3 simple but significant questions

           1. does anyone know which direction south is?
           2. do you know where the closest chinese take
out is?
           3. which way is Ave. A?   i
answered then all.

By the Sky Rain Black Tears

Iris Pérez Ulloa

Reds tears,
blood's tears,
hunger's tears,
blacks tears . . .
Cry Got upon the world:
on the poor world
and on the rich world.
Cry Got
blacks tears
on the poors umbrellas,
on the brokens umbrellas,
on the shoeless foots
on the hunger and the misery
that support
our poor rich humanity.

DEL CIELO LLUEVEN LÁGRIMAS NEGRAS*

Lágrimas rojas,
lágrimas de sangre,
lágrimas de hambre,
lágrimas negras . . .
Llora Dios sobre el mundo:
sobre el mundo pobre
y sobre el mundo rico.
Llora Dios
lágrimas negras
sobre los paraguas pobres,
sobre los paraguas rotos,
sobre los pies descalzos
sobre el hambre y la miseria
que sostiene
a nuestra pobre rica humanidad.

Translation by author.

Satellite

MaryJo Martin

Circle
spinning round her
encompassing in reverse pieta.
Never out of site
though always at a distance.

What wisdom! How you bare uncertainty. Hold it with
a loose grip.
What wit!
But the price is heavy
when you feel powerless as observer.

And through the years
be they feast or famine
you maintain the same
lunar glow- her light reflected.

I might have to
cut you open
examine your ringed limbs
to measure your starvation.
And you would not cry.
You never have.

Strange glow of bone in moon.
Who will know how you loved her?
How you adored?

Who can hold such emptiness?
The trees are
anguished skeletons
open palms in sterile swamps.

The Great Quake of Sumatra-2004

Valery Oisteanu

Shiva the Destroyer striking without mercy
The Islands I loved, the beaches treasured in my memory
Leveled by quake and flood-like tsunami
The wrath of the Earth and the Ocean
Swiping floating Buddhas into the Indian Ocean
All the technology rendered useless by human indifference
Millions of cell phones, computers galore
But no one alert enough to send a message

Dead bodies hanging in the trees
Above the temples, above the mosques
The northern tip of Sumatra is gone
200.000 drawn and counting
I knew this people: Indonesian, Thai friends,
Indian and Ceylonese buddies
The last paradises I lived in are destroyed
Children swallowed by cruel dark waters
Nightmares on the "tourist beaches of perpetual sun"
Biblical floods in the lands of Islam
Travelers trapped in trains, busses and square rooms.

This is my recurring nightmare, chased by the waves
I am again a witness to the Divine Inferno
Watching bodies devoured by flames,
Buried in common-pits by bulldozers
No one can write poetry in the stenches of death
How powerless we feel in front of such devastation

Poetry dies with the children and the women and men
Floating in the somber sea, evaporating in smoke
The carved spirits and worshiped idols with bulging eyes
Watching the pyres of loved ones, no names, no good byes
Great Shiva, show your mercy at least for the sad-survivors
And forgive those that did not warn them on time
I will hold in my hands the shape of human dignity.

Nam Jai

—for my buddy Sudket missing while in Phuket during the tsunami.

Do you remember the trips we took
to the white sand beaches of Ilocos?
Do you remember the rainbow beach ball
you took from those Italian girls
and they chased you into the sea
and they removed your swimming trunks
and left you stranded waist deep in the ocean?
Do you remember drinking Mai Tais
and Tequila Sunrises in the afternoon
during long rainy days in Makati?

Those were our high school days
in Manila where you showed me how
they say thank you in Thailand
with a short bow, praying-like hands
touching the forehead. That is how I choose
to remember you, my dear friend,
your head slightly bowing
looking through the clear ocean water
for the smooth sandy bottom.

The Women Who Survived

H.T. Harrison

Sister, all the women killed
were wise, they knew
unwritten recipes and rituals

how to attend a birth
how to bury the dead

we know nothing, you said, we are weak,
why did we live, what will we do

Outside I watch
the three canoe paddlers in Polynesia
pitch and row through deep black sky

inside on a screen the real world
detaches those who die for it
from the mythmakers working to
silence all witnesses, those sound waves,

Sister, draw me back outside
only a small snake swallowing a mouse
a cat crouched in the ivy

as tectonic plate India slides under Burma

without warning on the screen
where is the seven-days-of-light prayer now

four weeks still counting the dead
how will you live without them

is the elixir in the poison
that white star of our imagining

the dead have only lost their bodies—
Tell them I am sorry. Talk to them.

Whatever the Sea

Anjana Basu

Whatever the sea takes
comes back again
dim green eyelids of shells
silk of mud
at high tide a stink of stranded fish, dead turtles.
Sharp sails slice the powdered tinsel
rolling among the stars

Heart

Sparrow

The heart is round,
or rather rounded—
not a sphere, but rounded.

Somehow, the heart
could not be a cube.

God wouldn't make
a cubical heart.

The Dark Continent

Teresa White

Africa, home of Lucy's bones
where is your heart?
Oldavi is scarred;
we can't stop searching.

You are the mother of us all,
eland romp in ten-thousand
year-old caves:

a lone hunter grasps a spear
which drips in burnt umber
down the crusted walls.

In Sierra Leone, survivors
learn to eat with their feet.
Why the butchery?
Where is your heart?

In Dafur, women tear thread
with their teeth to fashion tents,
water is scarce, there is no oil. Famine looks
over your shoulders with a greedy eye.

Capetown, O Cape of Good Hope,
where has hope gone? Your children
are orphaned, your best young men

and women dying.
O Africa, where is your heart?
When will your brown-eyed messiah come?

Waterloo Village

Patricia Roth Schwartz

mid-November, under low skies
I'm driving through the town
that founded Memorial Day down past
the VFW next to the laundromat
watching a woman whose face
I could find in a mirror
walk out to the curb bearing
an armful of branches.

This morning's body count
interrupts Haydn.

    I remember the days
of the Tet Offensive beamed in color
by satellite to the cramped dinette
where my parents sat eating, the beets
bleeding into the brussell sprouts,
their tiny bitter hearts.

        This Friday
under the Stars & Stripes the Vets
will be serving ziti: Families Welcome
the names of those not at the table
rest on the stone outside.

        When I was still
a spiral of cells, my father was shipped
to Italy. Men died
Men are always dying.

Women are always bearing
in their arms branches
still covered with leaves.

Jason Sanford Brown

the cockroach
feeling around with
one antenna

the many   the few

Marcielle Brandler

two foreign women talk to each other
in english   one with persian   one with korean
accent.
andy   lanky   coal   georgian   joins in
my argentinian students pester the cubans all in fun

i read to them   wounded knee   the moon
when horses shed their fur   the moon
when snow melts into tepees
man afraid of his horses   came to help
too late   too late

my bosslady is irish   brought by the church
she is white   i am white   i am indian   she is a nun
i am german   am french   am italian
but i am visibly white with no religion
with no quotations   with no celebrated book

opidi from kenya   with clay
dry in the cracks of his hands
this is my book
the niger dumping its evaporated water to the mississippi
these are my tracks
the stench of buffalo glands turning to humus
banditos robbing sand caravans my gothic ancestors
agnostic   adapted   this is my anthropogenesis

Praying to the Gods

Thaddeus Rutkowski

"Namaste!" I say reverently to the elders, and they say "Namaste!" back.
They say it even more piously than I do, because they've been saying it
for a long time. Since this is a greeting and we are in a temple, the elders
and I don't waste time on small talk. There are more important things to
do, like praying to each god individually, and this takes time. We're
addressing more than one god here, and each god is different, with his or
her own personality. I want my prayers to be heard, and I want to make
sure I know who I'm praying to.

Communicating with multiple deities takes some moving around, so I
take care to find the proper location. I don't want to get in anyone's way.
But as it turns out, on this day I can do all of my meditating in one spot.
All I have to do is take my place on the men's side of the temple. I
wouldn't venture to think what would happen if I didn't. All those indi-
vidual gods might become disturbed, and they might do something tem-
ple-shattering, something unholy, to punish my irreverence. So I don't
complain about the seating arrangement, at least not on this Tuesday or
Sunday.

The Last Wave

Michael Hillmer

the ripped tide
lapped by human sea recedes

the coast line broken
by a reflective foam of loss

people splintered by the shudder
of earth and water rising
to kiss the sky
steal them away
with Buddha's blood
on their lips

empty eye sockets fill up
with mud and skin
bursts open under wedding bands

extinct beings transfigure
into acts of love

beside the bodies of our species
we are made human again

These Bones Remember

Anthony Russell White

different skies, many landscapes, strange names, other faces,
remember when that earthquake split the Sacred Volcano,
spilling burning lava on our family, boiling these bones,
cannibals coming out of the night to take our children,
a single spear and a bone knife, inadequate defense,
my head and chest crushed in that sudden rock-fall
after a day of dismal hunting with four brothers,
being shaken violently, disjointed, then eaten
by some toothy feline I see but cannot name,
a fishing boat capsizing one Aegean night,
leaving seven widows on a distant beach,
the slow agony of childbirth gone awry,
with crying twins, and too much blood,
that musket ball burning in my belly
after the Battle of the Wilderness,
the coughing of aged infirmities,
with scrawny children watching,
inside wind-rattled hide tents
on some dusty, treeless plain,

Oh, yes, legions more.

This then is the truth death brings:
Other souls wore these bones—
bones are timeless—
Yes, there's a dying

an ending

silence

then new flesh for the old bones,
and a lifetime of dancing with a new partner.

Plaint

Aleda Shirley

Here, the sky to the north is a bright slate blue,
full of portent & ready to let go.
But it will not snow, the leaves have just peaked.
And the gingkos, the one by the library on State Street
& the one two houses down on Pinehurst,
know something; those leaves know the past is bright & warm
& can be held, briefly, aloft. But a night,
if not this one, then Thursday or Friday, will change
all this & the trees will spend their wealth recklessly

into the street & on to the lawns. *Ching ching ching:*
I'll hear it as I try to sleep, the sound of falling
beneath other sounds (a siren downtown, the cat
batting around his sisal mouse, my husband breathing),
like the canned song of winning under a casino's
din. And the next day someone will pay
someone else to rake them, blow them, bag them;
up & down the street black vinyl bags
that might be mistaken, from the distance of the sky,

for treasure washed up, bags of gold
swathed in seaweed. On the weather channel
scraps of azure mean snow is general in Kentucky.
For years I waited for dust to settle on the past
and dim the auric-rose of maple leaves
on a path in Cave Hill, to soften the tatted sleet
on the windshield of my old blue car, but this dust
is like that of a volcano, a lie, a lens distorting dawn
& sunset into lustre, for years after the event.

Beyond this Breath

Victory Lee Schouten

Your body must miss him so much.
Beyond the grief, no old age shared.

the small of your back must cry out
for his belly pressed up warm against,

his arm heavy around your hips
anchoring you here
with your children and grandchildren.

Beyond the shock of sudden death,
trying not to think of how scared
he might have been.

Beyond the silence
where his laughter used to live,

your sweet breasts must long
for his familiar hands
to hold their soft weight again.

Your lonely body listens,
impossible to believe
he won't be coming home.

Tonight I rub my man's shoulders,
memorize his spine with fingertips.
Mine. Mine for a breath,
so brief our time.

Just the time it takes
for a kitchen curtain to stir
in the evening breeze.

Moving to Higher Ground

Colette Jonopulos

—a haibun

Cape Perpetua, Oregon, January 2005

i.
We hike the cliffs above the ocean, the air ten degrees warmer here than inland. Sword ferns reach their spindly fingers toward our thighs and knees.

ii.
Pine needles, brown and flattened underfoot, release the scent of Christmas remembered: my father in his plaid robe belted at the waist, my mother's unruly hair, the waiting to open gifts while coffee brewed. What odd memories as we breathe heavily into the sea air, suspended above the Pacific, her waters calm and even.

this new year
we watch for whales
swimming south

iii.
Tsunami signs warn us to move to higher ground if a wave outgrows itself and pushes inland.

I imagine the ocean receding, and then growing beyond belief, beyond our ability to outrun its need to enfold.

a boy stacks
broken pieces of trees
limbs unearthed

iv.
The day after Christmas, along Asia's coast—tourists washed to sea with the locals. Thousands let go in unison; their unending silence haunts me still. I didn't watch television at first, and then huddled in pajamas for an entire morning with images of fishing boats and cars piled like discarded toys, miles of gutted land, bodies stacked for burning.

v.
The path off the loop trail is steeper than we'd thought; we force our-selves to continue upward to make it a five-mile hike. Our breathing is steady now, thoughts slowed to the rhythm of each footfall. We talk quietly

about our good fortune that it isn't raining, that there are so few people on the trails; we talk of anything but death.

vi.
A tree has split itself and fallen into the branches of another tree, crossing overhead. I take a photograph of its trajectory, the timing of it. As we climb higher, the slight sway of trees draws our eyes upward. Their wooden arms rub together; create the single keening sound of loss.

every March
gray whales swim north
calves in their wake

The Wall of Water

Lisa Ezzard

At his thatched shanty, in Cuddalore, India
a fisherman had dropped off some fish and said goodbye
to his three children and his wife.
Then, a few hundred years away, at his little boat,
He saw people run, he saw a wall of water taller than the trees,
He saw his family swept out to sea.
He held tight to a tree with roots.

I am watching the water carefully as I walk
The waves rising at the horizon
The cliffs locking me in on the beach
Back onto pavement
I imagine bloated bodies filling the streets
The floodwaters, in Band Aceh, flowing through a city hospital
Drowning its patients
I drop Bach flower water into my mouth
That holds the essence of red chestnut, Star of Bethlehem.

All of the fishermen who went out to sea have not come back
Nameless fishermen and fishing villages
There are no shells in this dim light,
not even a broken sand dollar
Whose debris bobs on the surface?
Whose bodies left in the branches of trees?

Look how the epicenter of the quake
radiates in concentric circles—
Banda Aceh, Phuket, Thailand, Andaman Islands, Nicobar Islands,
Sri Lanka,
Maldive Islands, Madras, Somalia, Mogadishu

Starbucks is closed at 5:00 am.
The 24-hour donut shop is closed.
I am walking home in pouring rain,
This projectile of tears.
After their massages at elite resorts
The foreigners are all washed away
A well-known fashion photographer
Has been draped in red cloth by the locals
Farmers and laborers lay in clusters
The great wall of water has opened a chaotic door
400 prisoners escape

60

So many women unable to outrun the sea
This one, a tag tied to her foot, #196
Women balance scraps in baskets
They are moving to high ground

The sea has taken even the traces of pictures
How can you, survivor, rebuild a small house
And live alone?
I have opened my Atlas
I am looking at the mass of Indian Ocean rim

The ocean here in Cardiff has risen 10 feet,
And it washes up to the edge.
I have risen, unlike any other night,
To walk the beach at 3:00 am.

Miracle*

Roberta Gould

There is nothing to do but
give to the poor
They abound as fish did
Even the division of bread
into crumbs gives something
for life to go on

The masters, indeed, have increased
the sea of the starving
the better to chain life
in their infinite greed
They do it with prayer
and a song

But their own children
are not deceived
Mad in luxury cages they cut
their arms and pierce their breasts
as the anthem plays "Thanatos, Thanatos"
the promised miracle.

*From *Artist in a Time of Hell*

The Slowly Disappearing Elephant in the Room

Alan Semerdjian

looks like your Armenian grandmother,
who warned of such, of leaving the door
ajar, or three green peas even
and the tv on after dinner.
And although some call it often,
others, several million more likely,
refer to it as dead, flooded in the blowhole,
its dim whale memory not enough
to surface and say, "What does it take?"
But some still see it, there, cornered
aghast, and wait to see it dissolve like
tabs of antacid in a glass, rub their mitts
as praying mantis stop to scream.
Others simply drop their heads
and walk past it in their sleep, their
feet wet with nightmare, their children
wrapped in nightgowns and fake sleep,
so when it finally leaves, there will be room
to mourn and replace with furniture
and thieves because in this world
of war and species, there are no zoos,
only zookeepers, and what they hold
is what you held once in a photograph, in a locket
your grandmother or the woman on tv
wore or kept beside her bed, next to the aquarium,
before that, too, disappeared.

Flooding Heaven

Kirpal Gordon

*Oceans are the subconscious of the world. Deserts are the waking
awareness. Everything counts in the desert. The word has enormous
power. Not what people mean but what they say. Intended meaning is
beside the point. The word itself is all that matters. The Hindu woman
tries to avoid speaking her husband's name. Every utterance of his name
brings him closer to death.*
—Don DeLillo, *The Names*

      If seven temptations are followed by a railway & one finds
oneself awake in a boxcar of light, why not admit one's destination to be
heaven, the end of every brilliance that begins as desire? In a speeding
train en route to the Arabian Sea one may have just undressed a lover or
a head wound to enter a rent of light so bright one felt oneself disappear.
Yes & how the straight-away roar of that engine raced west into a coastal
sunset with a sound to blast hollow all the sounds of a surrounding coun-
tryside! Only when day's last light seemed suspended could the train's
locomotion lull one into a dream, a dream only motion's sudden end
could awaken one from: waves from an ocean's mountain and everyone
dead. A locomotive's headlight floods the shadows a moon of white
roses bestows to reveal the damage, steel rails & human ribs broken from
their most certain parallels.

      Some say the desert herself walks backward in time, so wan-
dering the horizon may invite a prehistoric escort. Face it: having already
surrendered sanity one might follow any guide's lead out of explanations
into the cool width of the river whose curves in the earth resemble a
woman's moonlit profile, a shapeliness that draws the night wind into
song, a singing to torture everything left unloved. He may find himself
scaling a hillside of tall trees spread wide as the river bends to shade his
fever until what stood between him & not-him shed. In their canopy a
hot spring heaves, a heartbeat inside the earth. He needs only to crawl
forward to enter pools of water.

      Even the unborn wander across versions of paradise said to
cross one another in a moonscape carved this deep out of loss, so who
one is (witness to what the ancients built or just a sole survivor fleeing a
train wreck) is not dead so much as immaterial. Not to worry, not to fear.
This is what heavens are made from, what heavens were made for.

63

Something for the New Year

Donald Lev

How do I write something upbeat
for the new year? Not that I have
to. I've been told I'm never that
upbeat anyway. Hey maybe
threehundredthousand in Asia
killed by the tsunami and no
let-up in Iraq, whose horrors
seem dwarfed at the moment; and my
own loss a year ago, but a
loss for me every day of my
life: think of all those hundreds of
thousands of other everyday
losses, and then swing! How to sound,
not that I have to, up-beat, well
here I am posing the question.

You See How it Happened

Laura Foley

You see how it happened.
I lost a father, a mother.
I lost a husband.
My sons left me.
I was alone with a daughter
I could not see
in a house that had no foundation.
I was homeless.
I shuffled through streets, ate
from strangers' plates, wandered
on forest paths,
until the lamp of the world went out.
Obsessions faded.
I returned home, free in my mind.
From across the river, three tall boats were gliding in.

Surrender

Scott Wiggerman

She squats in the muck
at the water's edge
as she has for a week,
fixed to the spot
like a lighthouse

sinking.
Her weary eyes stare down
the cinnamon-colored sea,
as if willpower alone
could control its roil,

force it to return
the child she could not
cling to, cannot beacon—
or sweep the urge
from under her feet.

The Moon on the Tsunami

Kate Gray

The moon
a month ago
made silver
the water swallowing
your shore.
You didn't want
to see dark things
floating
in hoary light, what
rooftop, what
scrap, what
limb. Too cruel
that fullness
pulling the tide.

Years ago
the woman I loved
on the other side
of an ocean wrote notes
daily to say
the moon she saw
was the same one I saw,
walking under its thick light,
we were
inseparable.

After she
drowned, the moon
was all
I saw of her.

Tonight the full moon
is all flesh. Touch it
and you touch
what the ocean
took from you.

Gathering in the North Wind

Patricia Wellingham-Jones

for Kelly

He towers over the mourners
clustered near flowers
and fake grass. Bends
his head as if listening
to others speak. Eyes focused
on his armful of child in red,
it is her tiny voice
his ear cups to catch.
One large hand tugs the red hood
over her tousled hair,
envelopes her whole head
in tender palm.
Under his jacket a toy
black cat dangles, right arm
jammed deep in his pocket.
He, of all present,
is most aware of the cycle,
the yielding up of one generation,
fragile bloom of the next.

Come Here. Take Heart

Verandah Porche

1.
A pillow cradles her head.
Tears tilt
cool trails to the temples.
Into the blue and out of it
have fallen thousands
(thou to sand),
rich, poor and uninsured
who cast and reeled,
tilled, tended, or terrorized,
who beckoned
pale phototropic tourists
from the north
and welcomed them
to the fullness
of a body of water
the room temperature
of a heart.

2.
Come here.
From roots and *brassicas*, take heart,
from the hoarded warmth of August,
from creatures, named, crooned to,
raised to give, take heart;
from Price Chopper's
child or crone cashiers
and the Co-op's studded divas
and meditative baggers.

For ample time
above the simple friction
of our seismic faults;
for God or history who called
our feral cells to the high ground
where we find ourselves
without irony, let us
say grace.

Tsunami

I

On border of two
of tectonic plates
which carry like turtles
world's continents and oceans
9.0 magnitude slippage

II

Earth wobbles almost
inch on axis, spins three
microseconds faster

In all directions
seismic tide crosses Indian
Ocean at jet speed

"Sea is coming" warnings
Five feet high Islands
disappear for moment

Over blue resort waves
young prince's jet ski roars
Body buried in Bangkok

Furniture pushed out
hotel lobby . . . car pulled in
and turned upside down

Passengers watch waves
cover tour bus. . . .
New driver and destination

Jacob wrestles Neptune
to keep son in embrace
This time, gods prevail

Time for debate ends
Decide, Mother, which child
lives and which one dies

Bodies pulled from mounds
of concrete and mud "More
coming," old woman yells

Corpse wearing bra . . . smaller
one in striped tee shirt . . . Boy
throws stone at ocean

Woman escapes to forest
where son is born
He's called Tsunami

III

Parents without kids
and recent orphans ask
what wrong has been done
to justify all this grief?
Fools rush in to answer

total eclipse, new year: 2005

Eve Packer

THE DOGS CAN
    feel it
she says
    talking abt
hurricanes
    It was an
earthquake i say
    Earthquakes
too she
    says

Naked in
    the steam room,
but for sable eyeliner,
   kneading huge breasts & belly,
in her 70's, i'm from lithuania
       she says, my husband, moscow

You live such
   a long time
   she says you
never know

what will happen—
as long as it
doesnt happen
      here
she pauses
in America—do you think?

It will i say, then,
   probably,
            add,
Happy New Year

i can see her on the warm sand
in phuket, surrounded by dogs,
facing the receding tide, and she sees
the dogs sniffing, or they start barking, running
after their own tails, they FEEL it, she says,
and starts shouting, waving her big arms,
warning bathers beach-strollers villagers, and everyone,
all 130—150—170—220,000, even—especially—the children, are saved

What's Left

Taylor Graham

As if shipwrecked here
for a week of summer
on an island
washed by earthquake water,
not another human being
here alive,
we walk the tsunami line.
Weathered bones flung
so far above high-water
Shells like small caskets
on the tide.

I've Come Down From The Peak

Roger Aplon

where hollyhocks no longer bloom & engines run amuck & the view of
your mountain is lost to time. I've come

with arms full of nettles & burrs & briars stuck to my leggings where a
blue boar nurses the gypsy kids & eats their enemies whole.

I've seen it gnaw the leg of an insolent peasant & the face of a county
cop & I've slept in its den & washed its feet & combed its stinking hair.

There's not much time or so they've told me & I want a drink of clear
water & a taste of ginger on my tongue.

Teach me to sleep again & teach me to hold on with both my hands –
there's a home long deserted & no one to turn the key.

Shadows Of Melancholy

Susan Norton

Beyond mortar and metal to safety,
my hair, soaked in disaster, my body,
drugged by soggy news bulletins.

Searching for relief, mute as a fish,
uttering only bubbles, I withdrew
into a sinkhole of silence.
Depressed blood is voiceless.

Wake Up, Little Sister

Ruth Knafo Setton

You ate the nine small
mice, fed rice to a corpse,
and collected moon foam
in a jar. You walked back
wards through the market,
back through your life, past
the orange tree. Past Papa beating
Maman, and Uncle sleeping
with your sister, down the valley,
south and west into the screaming
desert where the Tall Men crouched.
They made you a bed of sand, little sister,
that curved like a wave, enfolded your hips.
You lay staring at the black sky —

answers swept past you —
forked garden, masked women,
children who laughed
with flame lips, sun ray buried
beneath tiles.

The sea glittered, yellow-eyed,
as you stepped over the cliff.

You can't sink: too full of moon foam;
can't die: too stuffed with mouse hearts;
can't make a sound: dead
grains crowd your tongue.

Curve

R.M. Engelhardt

As nightfall starves the sun
another day ends, and into
evening

dusk.

The wheels roll, the engine hums,
children dream in shadows.
And the radio plays a familiar song
reminding two of when

they became one.

She smiles as she drives
He looks down at his watch

looks up.

The cross on the dashboard
frees Jesus, glass floats.

In the early morning hours
A small deer in a nearby wood

feeds.

The Orphans of Tangshan

Colette Inez

*After the earthquake of 1976 numerous
children, found in the rubble, were too young
to know their family names.*

The thunder has no mother.
Who is the father of the wind?
In the sky the Mother of the Seven Stars
gives honey to The Bear.
The orphanage children begin to speak.

A boy mutters earth has swallowed
his name and points at the ground.
Ghost sister, a girl shouts in her sleep.
The land ate my house, she says when she wakes.

After the earthquake, they are given new names.
Who are your parents? Visitors ask
and, do you love the party and the state?
Our teachers, they reply and yes, yes.

Calendars are hung and curled into scrolls,
quilts open and fold. Each day bowls
fill up with rice, white as the paper
that holds brushed words.

Years crumble and fall down, the children
get up and grow tall yet many keep stumbling
into dawn when the city of Tangshan
eases out of sleep and across the northern valley
mothers call Moon Willow, Monkey,
time to wake.

On Water

Rayn Roberts

Dasol Temple, South Korea

1. How Mind   Moves

The splash of water on rocks

                                                            at the high end

vibrations move, ripple the surface
but not the deep calm,
a center of lotus and lily pads
like a quiet deep of sea,
but water arrives by many ways
to be a pond: fed by mountain-top rain
seeping to a circle of stone
where deer drink
turtles sun and dream white and gold
orange and black carp
rising and falling like ideas
frogs in a daze
noon is only notion here and slowly
at low end, the water flows out
mind twisting in memories, a creek
turning through pines,
senses thought concept reason
enter the high end in noisy waves

leave the low, fulfillment

                                                            running to the

sea

2. Paradoxical

What we need for life
can be our death as well,
water, one moment
pleasure, then a hell:
The twisted body of a girl
on a shore of *Paradise*...
          empty as a shell.

aftermath

Michaela A. Gabriel

the sea is calm today;
no greedy fingers licking the sand,
no more driftwood, no flood
to wash away bad dreams

further inland, a temple
neglects all the gods of Tamil Nadu,
incense traded for rice,
songs for silent tears

amid stacks of clothes
more colourful than Rajasthan,
Jayashree cries for a mother
who has "gone east" --

a lie to protect a little girl;
in the east, dead fish litter beaches,
stunned mouths open, tail-fins crushed,
no-one will gather them

tangled in treetops,
papa's net bulges with strange fruit -
unclaimed harvest, pink-cheeked
as his unclaimed daughter

among windowless ruins,
the sun plays peek-a-boo in vain:
Jayashree's laughter lies drowned
on the ocean bed

fronds caressing the debris,
palm trees bend to the ground
and all the flowers grow
in faraway gardens

A Dirge for Two-Hundred Thousand

Ravi Shankar

for the Tsunami victims, 2005

The earth, like its inhabitants, is stitched
together in pieces, plates that rift in time
and might move a centimeter in a year,
else suddenly judder fifteen meters in half

a second, triggering walls of water
that first recede like the intake of breath,
exposing glistening kelp, convulsive fish,
sedimentary curiosities that draw onlookers

on when they should be fleeing for high ground,
that then accelerate to Lear jet speeds,
overflowing the shore in hissing torrents
to uproot trees, topple minarets, smash

sewers, tear railroad trestles into snarls
of metal, splintering, rending, dragging
object or person with such force no formula
can fathom, no theologian explicate,

though they will try-for the Buddhist,
everything is impermanent
except Dharma and one never knows
when the next wave may come;

for the Christian, forces of nature exist
to punish the unrighteous;
for the Hindu, reincarnation's wheel
spins from destruction to creation

and back again, until all humans,
eventually, rejoin the celestial;
for the Muslim, the Divine Essence
is immanent and beyond imagining,

forbidden for us even to ponder;
for the Humanist, suffering is incidental
to the molten core at the center of the earth.
For the Sri Lankan child who has lost

her family, whose school has been razed,

the rice paddies she helped cultivate
submerged in fetid water, the village
littered with glass-shards, car parts,

the rotting carcasses of dead dogs,
none of these explanations suffice.
Only the earth, unlike its inhabitants,
unlike us, has nothing to fully recover.

White Diamonds

Prasenjit Maiti

Your white chiffon burns as the sky burns in Calcutta and I dig inside
molten sundae and ketchup like religion like recluse like fantasy, your
white chiffon burns as I admire the riverfront and the bridge girdled like
chastity, the breeze and its fragrance like a woman in season and panting,
your white diamonds burn like your eyes, black like Bengal's sorrows and
ranting, your white diamonds burn like ashes like Coventry like merry sex
like royalty

In the Arms of Water

Sharon Olinka

The rushing movement gives. Takes away.
I have no more offerings. Tinsel
for gods. Or idealistic words.
Then further shocks. Bodies impaled
on trees. Bloated fish on sand.
Children who ate breakfast
that sparkling day, I see you
without ceasing walk back
and forth under banana
leaves. Stranger,
who gave me a rose
in Kanchipuram, are you still alive?
Time stopped for me
to the sound of a river.
It's greenish-silver.
But for you, all of you,
there's only ocean. The nourishing wave
that turned upon itself,
and in one crush,
destroyed dreams.

Disaster Relief

John Gorman

Pots and pans
shards of glass and mangled shirts spit up onto shore
atop
decaying bodies
as Vikram spins in
jagged circles
jumping over scabby limbs
till he is tugged from his
lofty heights
and
dragged toward a crowded table
littered with children
where the social worker
pushes a bowl of Fruit Loops in his general direction.

Follow the Directions on Page 226

Jennifer Hill-Kaucher

I imagine the woman in a paisley dress
or sarong. The man with one lost arm
will wear a white gauze shirt, or a jacquard
like a crossword. I can't tell if the brown enmeshed
between them is a baby or a porch ornament.
I want to pop them out of this shoreline of shards
imagine the woman, smooth each edge of her limbs,
turn the page, find her husband's briefcase, cut away
the table where they share dinner, recite prayers
that give thanks, fold the tabs around their backs
before the shoes at the ends of my fingers cement.
I imagine the woman.

"Pass The Sugar"

Gregory Miller

Twelve miles away,
trees fall in twisted seizures
across roads, crush against homes,
leaves ripped into the phantom grip
of midnight storms.
The roads funnel waters.
Funnels funnel air, three seen in
four minutes.

Children, as later reported,
scream toward the sudden infinitude of ceilings
now made of sky.

An office trailer slides,
bright tons of hulking chrome pallor,
forty-eight feet across five lanes of highway.
Inside, three women hunt for faith before
one awakes, blinking at the lights of her hospital room,
oblivious of the colder room next door
where others stare and stare.

Long hours later, a couple's good sleep finds
new depths of meaning in the light of
a cloudless morning darkened by ink
that cannot, by its nature, bode well
for pleasant breakfasts.

But newsprint pages turn.
Coffee slurping voices
giggle at comic strips.

"Last night," someone says,
"The candle beside the bed did not flicker."

"Pass the sugar."

The Moon Will Claim Me

Diane di Prima

savagely
a black thing
swooping down
just the way it would
at the edge of the roof

I didn't choose this destiny.
My living room mirror is like a fish tank
and I'm growing silver scales.

By the ocean
calm, peaceful
not wearing shoes or socks
I call my father.

How could I have forgotten?
I always knew what time
I had to leave.

like white crumpled paper
floating down the street

While You Were Sleeping

George Wallace

the earth turned left the earth turned right the axis of the planet
churned like butter
while you were sleeping the soil grew silent the sea grew
cautious the sky grew omnivorous
cows and humans ran for their lives, blackwidow spiders
climbed to the tops of trees
bituminous coal fell like liquid diamonds from the mouths of
furious strangers
plants like dinosaurs shook the land, sheep like lizards shed
their wool
a man and a penguin and a quarter moon orbited the gates of
heaven
while you were sleeping rocks grew envious air turned
poisonous
gods grew ravenous the blue impossible waves of oceans fought
each other
in the eyes of the innocent the wind blew bigger than the lies of
presidents
the rain blew hotter than tanks the sand blew wider than
armored vehicles
while you were sleeping sleep-engines rattled, spin-wheels
moaned
plates and saucers in the cupboard of familiar places shattered
to pieces
an automobile which had been hired to plunge off the edge of a
movie cliff
plunged off the edge of an actual cliff - it fell and fell deep into
a rocky ravine
there was a wedding party inside it and a flock of crows and
julia roberts
oh yeah, she was in it! and a cockroach and a pair of stockings
and an ozone hole
a pair of out of work actors on their way to las vegas nevada
was in it too
someone told them things were better in las vegas than they were
in hollywood—
they heard it on the radio, so it must be true. they all burned up
in the famous flames.

Hush

Katherine Tracy

Poison oak clings,
foraging unfolded branches.
He whittles a wooden creed,
twirling jagged leaves onto bark.
Raw timber jabbed indiscreetly,
chilling growth where untended dreams die.

Harsh hard hush, winter slows green,
listening as my father's child,
untilled dormant bud,
like a stripling lass who lingers,
calling blackberry winter.

Beyond bittersweet blankets
snowflakes melt, refreshing rivers flow.
A blossom echoes the first spring rain
spooling hills in the vernal season
        of my daughter.

Bells for Mindfulness

Thomas J. Baier

1.
The day opens like a snap pea,
Becomes
A string of memory pearls
Milky as myths
Words over words
Day building a month
Month growing a year
With curling around without.

2.
The waiting is not how you imagined it.
Soon you'll erode
And fall
In an underwater landslide
From the gravity of what you haven't done
To pearl in your secret oyster
Of silent complaint.

3.
We loiter silly in the waiting pools
Of what we do
Blissful as school children picking shells off the beach
At sea level
Below sea level.
The sky has the face of a flounder
Who was born upright but learned
To swim sideways
To hide.
The sun is a scorpion god riding a pyramid
Momentarily more beautiful than what we can afford,
New.

4.
But your rent is now due
So you'll have life here again
After the cleanup, after the charity, after the rebuilding,
The repaving, the repainting
And your actions will be the only property
You'll ever own.

For You

Craig Czury

one same moment as earth
in our love cries
or death cry
the quake of our bodies
gasping

Not Our Sea

Jennifer Browne

"Disaster changes use of word tsunami"
  -*Global Language Monitor*

Musicians once produced a sonic tsunami
and Wall Street analysts foresaw tsunamis
of bad earnings while Japanese restaurants
served up tsunami rolls. Even the tag stitched
inside my pants reads tsunami so I'm wearing
the word at the sacrum, word flat to the bone
once thought to make people rise from the dead.

So where's the man who seeks small Thai hands
to unzip the muscles of his back and beaches
where his name isn't Stan, Assistant Manager?
He used to spread his vacation photos across
the break room table, lean in close and point
*see here's where you can really
get a sense of the size of this…*

The baby whose face is tacked to every tree
in Sri Lanka   *ten months   two small teeth, beneath?*
Beneath, with the rest of the fisherman's words
leaving only
this is not our sea.
Tsunami, rise and fall of a word
that sounds so close to you not me. See

I can't get a sense of the size of this
can't press my finger onto the two
still half-buried rocks on the reef
of my baby's gums and imagine
              as when she says *my baby's body like oil and I can't hold*
as when he says *the sea disappeared then*
as when they all say *wall of wall of wall of*

I once found the perfect angle
so the deck rail traced the horizon line
and the sea became the sky and I'm sorry
for ever thinking it beautiful. As in pleasing
to the eye. As when my husband tells me
my pictures have too much sea and sky and how
I should always try and get a person in there.

An Argument With Memory

Marge Piercy

You are something I drag behind me
in the dust like a peacock's tail
sweeping up leaves, ignored
until something prompts that display:

then the dull weight of the forgotten
spreads out a glorious fan
iridescent flightless feathers shining,
and the hundred eyes reporting.

Yes, memory, you are this weight
I lug about like an oversized briefcase,
like a too big too full suitcase
pulling my shoulder from its socket.

You are my shadow that weighs
more than lead. You turn on
in the night and your searchlight
vanishes the present and sleep.

I study how to make you more vivid,
stronger, and you suck me under
into viscous cold black waters
where my body too remembers,

opens lost gills and I breathe
your thick substance and you take
over my brain and instruct me
how to serve in the synagogue-

library-catacombs of your power.
Ah, you say, what could be weaker
than me, who reside in splinters,
in grandmother's tales, in fading

brown photographs, in evanescent
scents of tulip and black bean soup,
weak as a taper until you light
my flame with your mind.

Kaira Peace

as sung by Papa Susso to Bob Holman

Kaira is a word
It is the word for Peace
Kaira means Peace I think you can hear that
Kaira Oh how Papa Susso loves that word Kaira
Papa Susso, the Internet griot with a BA degree
It is such pleasure to sing Kaira up and down kora strings
Listen to Kaira, that pleases peace, Please Peace Now
Slavery is over, that's what peace means
1945, West Africa, you know the World War
Was happening Kaira but in West Africa,
In Senegambia, 1945 was the year slavery was abolished
No more slaves means peace Kaira!
Now it so happened that a few years later
There was a rich man in Guinea
Name of Kaira-ba Toure, his name
Was Peace and he loved Peace so it was all together
And there was a great great great balafon player, I'm talking
Teneng Sory Diabate, who saw this and rededicated Kaira
To this patron of the arts and this patron of Peace, Kaira, Kaira-ba

Now listen here is Kaira

Slavery abolished but people still fight for power, Kaira
The jeli sing Kaira and people who come from the slave families,
Well, they still call themselves slaves, they walk around
Only now they follow no one. They are looking for work like everyone
else.
And the power struggles you could say they go on to this day
This New Year Day let's know this word Kaira
It's a word for Peace, it pleases peace, Please Peace Now
With slaves in Mauritania and Sudan — Kaira
With political prisoners in US and Eritrea — Kaira
With people dying in Iraq even though the war is not a war — Kaira
The kora plays the contradictions and plays for Kaira, for Peace
That is Kaira, the word for Peace
Please Peace Now
Kaira is the word for Peace

unholy waters

Gerald Schwartz

creating ceaseless

absences

at the base of

now

boundless ends

angels lost

in this bottomless—

proof

no mater what

all can be

unmattered

instantly.

It Was Apparent To the Orphans

Amy Ouzoonian

Collapsing all hope
to pull you over my back,

Gathering your pearl face
swinging in a tsunami-afghan-
hammock—a bed
for your last night.

We ask the usual questions:
how many arms held you,

how many toes kicked your wombless torso;
who dressed your hair and lips
                                        in rose water,
who   loved your eyes hollow;

how many mothers, fathers, aunts,

half cousins and step-siblings
share your grave now.

When a person ceases to be   counted
—when they have
washed inland and

become the rumored island
glass sanded to tremor and wave,
numbers
call them onto paper and say,

"We're sorry, but
we have no record of your memory here,
please go to the back of the line
and wait
for the next man-made disaster."

The Stream

Dale Edmands

for Mark Strand

If you stand here
long enough,
stand here
at the edge
where it flows
past you
in a hurriedness
of splash
and roll,
of white foam
over rock,
of wave
after wave,
you begin
to understand
that this
is your life,
and there
beneath
the surface
where the sun
glitters with
aquatic stars
are the smiles
you gave;
all going by
in a rush
down there
under the bridge
and around
that last bend
disappearing,
and if you
follow,
you will
disappear
with it
and become
these black
rocks
the water

runs white
over,
like rain
in a graveyard
of wet, polished
stone

We Were On a Train and the Train Screeched

Lyn Lifshin

we thought it was someone
stepping in front of the
train to kill themselves.
This happens often

Then I saw the wave
coming against the train.
I put my daughter on
the luggage rack. Then,

a noise like a bomb.
I forget everything else.
Next I saw a child's
shoe, a grade school

report card. Babies'
shoes. We were the only
two in our car
to live.

Aftermath

Selene Steese

I saw them, finally.
The photographs I had been
avoiding for weeks. I'd seen
pieces on the television,
turned it off before grief
guillotined my defenses,
swept away my decorum
like a mammoth wall of water.

I'd read the stories, wept,
sent money, put the stories
aside when panic rose
at the thought of death descending
from scrubbed blue tropical
morning skies, at the thought of life
snuffed out just as it is waking
to the sun and wonder
of the world.

I saw the photographs, at last,
in a magazine—of the water
approaching, of people
beginning to flee, and one man
poised for flight, his lean body
bunching, telling him
run, run, death is coming,
his face turned toward disaster,
The camera did not record his look—
of disbelief? Of horror? Of panic warring
with wonderment? Of peace, acceptance—
perhaps, I've led a good life
and here's the end; so be it?

The other photographs—of devastation,
of bodies, of rescue operations,
of bodies, of grieving mothers, of bodies,
of mass graves, of makeshift morgues,
of survivors waiting for news, of bodies,
of bodies, of bodies. Someone

calls my name. I blink, blink, begin
to surface, to breathe—I look up. The woman

95

is ready to cut my hair. I

put the magazine aside, rise
from my sun-warmed
vinyl chair. Life
and its mundanities are calling.

I blink, blink in the winter
afternoon sun. Life
and its mundanities are calling.

How grateful I am to have
this moment. How infinitely,
unfathomably blessed.

Juanito Escareal

all day long,
rising from the temple
flocks of grey herons

Crying in My Heart

Fofana M.L.

My garden of fire!
Full of mushrooming roses,
Competes with eternity.
March and August have no venom
To storm the construction of my heart.
Thinking of my eye.

But the reception accorded to unknown visitors,
That come to prey and dissolve,
Has left scars deepened by the fruits
That know no logic, death or age.

Were this a passenger
That alights and reverses the course,
What happens under the sky is trivial
When my eye is my soul.

Basket Of Figs

Ellen Bass

Bring me your pain, love. Spread
it out like fine rugs, silk sashes,
warm eggs, cinnamon
and cloves in burlap sacks. Show me

the detail, the intricate embroidery
on the collar, tiny shell buttons,
the hem stitched the way you were taught,
pricking just a thread, almost invisible.

Unclasp it like jewels, the gold
still hot from your body. Empty
your basket of figs. Spill your wine.

That hard nugget of pain, I would suck it,
cradling it on my tongue like the slick
seed of pomegranate. I would lift it

tenderly, as a great animal might
carry a small one in the private
cave of the mouth.

Untitled

Denis Emorine translated in English by Pradip Choudhuri

One day, we've turned up to say no to death. She stared at us from a distance, bending the heavy nape of our neck. She has always followed us, even if, sometimes, she shows up with the sparks of life, a dreadful masque.

I never at all mention her name except when she explodes on others' life: that matters.

Through the drowsy nights, she moves in her guise, fingers on the lips of the persons asleep.

I hate her intrigues.

Nous sommes apparus un jour pour dire non à la mort. Elle nous dévisageait de loin, courbant nos nuques alourdies. Elle nous a toujours suivis même si, parfois, elle se parait d' éclats de vie, masque redouté.

Je n' arrive toujours pas à la nommer sauf lorsqu' elle éclate sur la vie des autres: ceux qui comptent.

A travers les nuits ensommeillées, elle circule à sa guise, le doigt sur les lèvres des dormeurs.

Je la hais d' agir.

Translator's note: Death, "la mort" is feminine in French. So I've used "She" instead of "it."

Excerpts from "Justice Because"

Jesus Papoleto Melendez

Where once proud peasants toiled the land—
                                       Pity them now,
   For woe are they and their backward way of life,
      hands-on with nature, as it were;
                             Their loss fails to bring a tear
to swell
                                  in the socket
of a glutton's eye;
For decisions are made in well hidden, higher places
                               Somewhere near
God's house,
Wherein ultimately it is decided which esoterically indigenous real estate property
will take a tumble in a cloud of mud and dust into the oceans' floor,
opening new opportunistic doors for the development of beach-front bungalows
for the newly rich from war to exploit & their kids explore.

While life remains lonely and so full of desolation for those whose lives
fall down ugly, more or less destitute from birth, such attests to their own worth
That not a fickle finger is lifted, nor shared the wealth of knowledge
of how to make ends meet in Paradise—
                               Right here, right now!
   To shift the unequal weight of human misery on the planet Earth.

But because, unlike the strongest trees, Men will not
by a subtle breeze be swayed from the joy of their misdeeds—
They are the branches that do not yield to the winds of time,
and therefore break by the weight of their own stubbornness.

So Everyone, as promised, will receive their turn to die . . .
   And they'll be awarded at that time
                         both, a Birth and Death
Certificate,
                     without much 'Thanks'
                       for their participation in
this Life.
And when the Earth itself finally dies,
                   only a certainly selected,
intelligent
   Insect will remain,

to bit, by bit, pick up the pieces once again,
and reorganize the world anew;
And to prove once more, that
No one alive has yet
removed

the dust from

his own grave.
Thus, it is GOD,
Ultimately, who is to blame
For it is He who must love the misery that He so often keeps.

Clear White Stream

Marilyn Chin

Clear white stream—
a dead horse drifts;
its legs are branches
piercing the sky.

Clear white stream—
a child dangles her pole;
deep in the water
a lungfish bites.

Clear white stream—
a man mooring a boat;
his cormorant is diving
with rope around its gullet.

Clear white stream—
a ripe red sun
drags its head
across the hollyhock.

Clear white stream—
how all will pass:
days and nights,
one horse's demise.

Clear white stream—
above my forehead
blue flies tarry
around a naked bulb.

Clear white stream—
am I river or horse,
man or cormorant,
woman or child?
Am I Chuangtzu's bad dream
shorn of an awakening?

Salomon Mercado

Nancy Mercado

Have seen you
Make the best of things
Offer a good word
To a friend in the street
A dollar for charity
While you were in need

Seen you physically broken
Paralyzed burned and mended
Wrapped in white bandages and casts
While all along coaxing us for laughs

I've seen you place your needs
Second to your family's
Sweat for twenty-six years
Labor in industrial kitchens
To secure a shelter for our lives

Have seen you volunteer your days off
To scrub the town's chapel
To visit the sick and deceased
To give comfort to the poor
You thought were poorer than you

Seen you take-in your elderly mother
Open the doors of our home for friends
Tread softly wherever you stepped

I saw you offer-up endless prayers for our world

Biographies of Authors

Diane Ackerman is a poet, essayist, and naturalist, and the author of twenty books of poetry and nonfiction, including most recently *An Alchemy of the Mind* (prose) and *Origami Bridges* (poetry).

In 2002, Medium Rare Books released *Biting Midnight: A Feast of Darksome Verse*, **Maria Alexander's** dark poetry collection with Christina Kiplinger-Johns. http://www.thehandlesspoet.com.

Lucy Anderton is the Virginia Center For The Creative Art's Artist-in-Residence in Auvillar, France. She has work forthcoming in *The Iowa Review* and *American Letters & Commentary*.

Roger Aplon has published four books of poetry along with miscellaneous poems stories in print and on the web. His latest collection, *Barcelona Diary* is in English & Catalan. Visit his website: www.rogeraplon.com.

Brett Axel is a Unitarian Universalist, a social and political activist, and a three time Woodstock National Slam Team member. His books include *First on the Fire* (Fly By Night), *Will Work For Peace* (Zeropanik Press) and *Disaster Relief* (Minimal Press).

Thomas Baier studied poetry at The State University of New York at Binghamton and was awarded The George R. Dunham Poetry Prize. Tom received his MA in English from The State University of New York at Stony Brook in 1993 and has worked continuously at both Herricks High School and Molloy College since 1994.

Ellen Bass's most recent book of poetry is *Mules of Love* (BOA LTD Editions). Among her awards are the Lambda Literary Award and a Pushcart Prize. Her non-fiction books include *Free Your Mind* and *The Courage to Heal*. She teaches poetry and creative writing in Santa Cruz, CA. www.ellenbass.com.

Anjana Basu poet, journalist and short story writer has been published in e-zines and print journals worldwide. She is a Hawthornden Fellow and her recent novel is *Curses and Ivory* (Harper Collins, India). Her new novel *Black Tongue* is forthcoming.

Natasa Bozic Grojic comes from Belgrade, Serbia and Montenegro. She has a BA in English language and literature. She works as a teacher of English. She writes poetry and short stories, both in English and in Serbian.

Marcielle Brandler has published poems since 1976. She writes for local newspapers and was editor for *Religion & Ethics Digest* and *Working Title* and Entertainment Writer for *Creative Line Magazine*. She has her own public access TV show with Adelphia TV and will appear in *Who'sWho*. www.webspawner.com/users/marcielle/

Jenny Browne writes and lives in a hundred year old house in downtown San Antonio, Texas. Her first collection of poems, *At Once*, was published by the University of Tampa Press in 2002. She is the editor of *Provide and Protect: Writers on Planned and Unplanned Parenthood* (Wings Press 2005).

Nick Carbo is the author of three books of poetry, including *Andalusian Dawn* (2004). He teaches in the MFA graduate writing program at the University of Miami.

David Chorlton was born in Austria, grew up in England, and spent several years in Vienna before moving to Phoenix in 1978. His book *Return to Waking Life* is from Main Street Rag Publishing Company.

Ray Craig was born and raised in Tokyo, Japan. He currently resides in San Bruno, California. Recent online works can be found at: *Big Bridge, Issue 10* and *Leevi Lehto's Google Poetry Engine*.

Craig Czury is a poet who works in schools, prisons, homeless shelters, mental hospitals and community centers. His books have been translated into Russian, Spanish, Lithuanian, Portuguese, Italian and Croatian. He lives in Reading, PA, and edits Zoo5 Int'l poetry pamphlets.

Steven Dalachinsky's most recent books include *trial and error in paris* (loudmouth collective press) *in glorious black and white* (ugly duckling press), and the soon to be released *trust fund babies* (pitch-fork press). His work is also in the anthology *The Outlaw Bible of American Poetry*.

Diane di Prima lives and works in San Francisco, where she teaches privately. Her recent books are *Loba: Books I and II*, and an autobiography, *Recollections of My Life as a Woman*, both published by Penguin. This Fall, Last Gasp Press will publish a new edition of her *Revolutionary Letters*, which will include 23 new poems. In 2006 Penguin will issue *Opening to the Poem*.

Dale A. Edmands is the Webmaster for *Kookamonga Square*, an online Literary and Art Collection. His work has been published widely online and in print.

Denis Emorine was born in 1956, near Paris. He is the author of short stories, essays, poetry and theater. One of his poemsbooks *No through world* (Ravenna Press 2004). http://denis.emorine.free.fr

R.M. Engelhardt is a poet & writer currently living in Albany, NY. His work has been published previously in *The Georgetown Review*, *Thundersandwich*, *Sure!: The Charles Bukowski Newsletter* & many others.

Juanito Escareal is a haiku and tanka poet. His works appear in *Fuyoh/Rose Mallow* haiku quarterly magazine and other e-zines and tanka publications, notably *In the Ship's Wake*, a tanka anthology published in 2000.

Lisa Ezzard is an established poet, teacher, and dancer who has published children's poetry yearly for the past five years. Her work has been published in such literary journals as *Appalachian Heritage* and *Squaw Valley Review*.

Laura Foley has been published in various online and print journals. She lives and writes on the banks of the Connecticut River, in Cornish, NH, and is completing three manuscripts of poetry.

Michaela A. Gabriel lives in Vienna, Austria, where she assists adults in acquiring computer and English skills. Her first chapbook *apples for adam* was published earlier this year.

Born and bred New Yorker **Kirpal Gordon** (17 books and pamphlets of fiction and poetry; see www.KirpalG.com for more) ghostwrites non-fiction for a living and tours with the Claire Daly Band, a jazz quartet.

John Gorman's work has appeared in *Thunder Sandwich*, *New Works Review*, *Numb*, *Olivetree Review*, *Rouse* and is forthcoming in *Sigla* and *Nth Position*.

Roberta Gould is the author of 8 published books, several of which are: *Dream Yourself Flying*, *Only Rock*, *Not By Blood Alone* and *In Houses With Ladders*. A member of Pen International, she is working on 3 new volumes and on her collected poems.

Taylor Graham is a volunteer search-and-rescue dog handler. She's included in the anthology *California Poetry: Gold Rush to the Present*.

Kate Gray's chapbook, *Where She Goes*, chronicles mornings rowing on the river through Portland, Oregon, where she's lived for 20 years. She edits *Clackamas Literary Review*.

H. T. Harrison is a poet and essayist. Her recent books (poetry), published under the name Heather Thomas, are *Resurrection Papers* (Chax Press, 2003) and *Practicing Amnesia* (Singing Horse Press, 2000).

Jennifer Hill-Kaucher's second book of poetry, *Book of Days*, was published by Foothills Press in 2005. Her poetry has appeared in several publications such as *Agnieszka's Dowry*. She is a Pennsylvania Council on the Arts rostered poet and recently conducted a poetry residency in Ireland.

Michael Hillmer is the author of the book *Go To Heaven*. His poetry can also be found online at *About Poetry*, *Poets Against the War*, *Voices In Wartime*, and *Art-Arena World Poems*. He is an editor for *Moon Reader* and for *BeWrite.net Poetry*.

Bob Holman, proprietor of the Bowery Poetry Club. Bob's most recent CD is *In With the Out Crowd* (Mouth Almighty/Mercury); book, *A Couple of Ways of Doing Something*.

Alhaji Papa Susso is one of the Gambia's leading jeli (griots' keeper of the West African oral traditions). Papa's most recent CD is *Sotuma-Sere*, an extraordinary set of classic solo poems featuring his brilliant kora playing. Papa doesn't write books. He is one.

Colette Inez has authored nine poetry collections—most recently *Spinoza Doesn't Come Here Anymore* from Melville House Books—and has won Guggenheim, Rockefeller and two NEA fellowships. She teaches in Columbia University's Writing Program. Her memoir *The Secret of M. Dulong* will be published in 2005 by the University of Wisconsin Press.

Katherine James was a portrait artist living in the Philadelphia area with her husband and three children before entering Columbia's MFA program in writing. She is now at work completing her first novel.

Illustrator, **Barb Jernigan** was the Art Production Manager (and chief copywriter) for *The Edutainment Catalog*. Her published works include A *Rocking Horse Christmas*, which appeared in *Rosalind and Martin Greenberg's Christmas Bestiary*. Her drawings were most recently visible in *Grasslimb* www.grasslimb.com.

Jörgen Johansson is from Lidköping, Sweden. Started writing haiku, in Swedish, 2001, and in March 2003 he wrote his first one in English. Johansson has been published in many haiku publications, such as *Heron's Nest*, *Mainichi Newspaper*, Japan, *Ginyu Mag*, Japan, etc. He released two haiku books, *Cherry Blossoms* and *Sakura*, in 2003, of poets from around the globe.

Lois P. Jones has been published in *The California Quarterly* (Spring 2005) and in the anthology *Poets Gone Wild* by Lulu Press (forthcoming, 2005) as well as *Words & Pictures* on line.

Colette Jonopulos has two non-fiction books in print: *The One Thing Needful* and *Living Waters For a Parched Land*. Her poetry is in *Clackamas Literary Review* and *Rattlesnake Review*. She is currently co-editor of *Tiger's Eye: A Journal of Poetry*.

Laurie Klein's first book is *Bodies of Water, Bodies of Flesh*. She assisted with community development in a rural Thailand village in 2000. Her prose and poems appear in numerous journals and anthologies.

Ruth Knafo Setton is the author of the novel *The Road to Fez*. Born in Morocco, she is the recipient of literary fellowships from the NEA and PEN, among others. Her fiction, poetry and creative nonfiction appear in many journals and anthologies. She teaches at Lehigh University, where she's working on a new novel and a poetry collection.

Fofana M.L. is a graduate from Fourah Bay College, University of Sierra Leone. He was teaching and doing research on African Literature. He worked with the International Rescue Committee, in Guinea, a Humanitarian Relief Agency, to assist needy refugee children from Sierra Leone, Liberia and Ivory Coast.

Gary Lehmann teaches writing and poetry at the Rochester Institute of Technology. His essays and poetry are widely published. He is also author of a book of poetry entitled *Public Lives and Private Secrets* (Foothills Press, 2005).

Donald Lev has been writing and publishing poetry since 1958. His 13th collection, *Yesterday's News* (Outloudbooks, 2002), is obliquely about the WTC tragedy. He publishes/edits the literary tabloid *Home Planet News*, which he and his late wife Enid Dame founded in 1979.

Texas Review Press is publishing **Lyn Lifshin's** *The Licorice Daughter: My Year With Ruffian*. Her recent book of poems, *Another Woman Who Looks Like Me* is published by Black Sparrow. www.lynlifshin.com

Helen Losse is a poet with work in several print and web journals and a Poetry Co-Editor for *The Dead Mule School of Southern Literature*. Her chapbook, *Gathering the Broken Pieces*, is available from FootHills Publishing. She also writes book reviews for the *Winston-Salem Journal*.

Prasenjit Maiti is an Indian creative writer. His work has been extensively published in e-zines and print journals around the world. He experiments in prose poetry.

A recent New Paltz graduate with a BA in History, **MaryJo Martin** has been writing poetry since kindergarten. Her first project was to describe her emotional being as an animal in rhyming form. She has been hooked ever since.

Tara L. Masih has been published in *Confrontation, Hayden's Ferry Review, Natural Bridge, Red River Review*, and *The Caribbean Writer*. Her essays have been read on NPR, and her prose was nominated for a Pushcart Prize.

Ameena Mayer is an activist, singer and writer. She has performed in various venues in British Columbia. She is also an English teacher in Vancouver and an MC for poetry events.

Nancy Mercado recently earned her doctoral degree. The author of *It Concerns The Madness* (Long Shot Productions), she has served as Editor of *Long Shot Magazine* for eleven years and is the author of seven plays.

Karla Linn Merrifield, widely published in American literary journals and reviews, is the author of *Midst*, a collection of nature poetry. She teaches writing at SUNY Brockport each fall.

Chelle Miko resides in the Finger Lakes region of New York. Her poetry publications include publications include *The North American Review*, *Poet Lore*, *32 Poems Magazine*, Anon, Valparaiso Poetry Review, *Nimrod*, *Rhino*, *Eclectica*, and *The Paumanok Review*.

Gregory Miller's poetry has been published most recently in *Rosebud*. His first novel, *Big Cicadas*, was published in 2003. His first collection of poetry, *Four Autumns* (Forthcoming, *FootHills*.) He teaches high school English in Pittsburgh, PA.

Susan Norton resides in Los Angeles, California. Her work has appeared in such publications as: *The Southern Poetry Review*, *Writer's World Magazine*, *Silver Quill*, *The Knews*. Norton also has co-authored a seven book Easy Reader series for children, *Pyramid Pal's Adventures In Eating*, to encourage healthy eating habits in kids.

Irene O'Garden's poetry has found its way to the Off–Broadway stage (*Women On Fire*), hardcover (*Fat Girl*) and children's books (*The Scrubbly Bubbly Car Wash*, *Maybe My Baby*) as well as in many literary journals. www.ireneogarden.com.

Valery Oisteanu is a writer-artist who was born in Russia, (1943) and educated in Romania. He is the author of 10 books of poetry, a book of short fiction and a book of essays in progress: *The Avant-Gods*.

Sharon Olinka's second book of poems will be published by Marsh Hawk Press in 2006. Her poems have recently been in *Poetry East*, *The Cafe Review*, and *Nth position*.

David Oliveira is a poet, writer, and editor living in Cambodia. He is the author of *In the Presence of Snakes*, co-author of *A Near Country: Poems of Loss*, and co-editor of *How Much Earth: The Fresno Poets*. He is also in the anthology *California Poetry: From the Gold Rush to the Present*.

Editor, **Amy Ouzoonian** received her BA in Journalism and Creative Writing for the Theater from SUNY New Paltz in May 2004. She is the editor of the critically acclaimed anthology *Skyscrapers, Taxis and Tampons* (Fly By Night Press, 1999) and author of *Your Pill* (poetry) (Foothills Publishing Oct. 2004). She has edited four issues of *A Gathering of the Tribes* magazine.

Eve Packer, a poet from ny, performs frequently, Packer has three poetry/jazz CD's, and from fly by night press, two books, *skulls head samba*, and the just published *playland poems* 1994-2004.

Iris Perez Ulloa, is a Spanish artist and writer. She is the author of several books and art education articles, *Carven*, *mail artist show yours bilds* and *ex-libris*. She has taken part in more than one hundred international arts exhibitions.

Marge Piercy is the author of sixteen collections of poetry. She has written sixteen novels, most recently *The Third Child* from Morrow/Harper Collins, who also published her memoir, *Sleeping with Cats* and will be publishing her new novel *Sex Wars* in December. A CD of her political poetry *Louder, We Can't Hear You Yet* is just out from Leapfrog Press, which also published her early poems *Early Grrrl* and co-authored with Ira Wood, *So You Want To Write: How to Master the Craft of Fiction and Personal Narrative*; the 2nd enlarged edition will be out late this year.

Based in rural Vermont since 1968, **Verandah Porche** has published two books of poems, *The Body's Symmetry* (Harper and Row) and *Glancing Off* (See Through Books). In 1998, the Vermont Arts Council awarded her a Citation of Merit.

Andrew Riutta lives in Michigan with his wife, Lori, and their daughter, Issabella. His poems have been featured in numerous online and print journals, as well as international anthologies. He has been writing for fifteen years.

Rayn Roberts appears in *Rattle, Rattapallax, The Sow's Ear Review, Thunder Sandwich, Pedestal Magazine, Poetic Voices, Voices in Wartime*, two Anthologies by Beyond Borders Press. www.geocities.com/raynrobkorea

Renée Roehl is a writer and an owner of a small business selling wild mushrooms. She lives with her son, partner, cats, dog and fish in Spokane, Washington.

Patricia Roth Schwartz has published widely in small press journals including *Nimrod* and *South Carolina Review*, and has a full-length volume just out from FootHills called *Planting Bulbs in a Time of War, and Other Poems*.

Anthony Russell White is a poet, a pilgrim, and a healer. He lives on a mountaintop in San Rafael, CA, with his wife, Daphne Crocker-White, and serves as a senior staff member for the Nine Gates Mystery School.

Thaddeus Rutkowski's novel, *Roughhouse* (Kaya Press), was a finalist for an Asian American Literary Awards. His work has been anthologized in *Screaming Monkeys: Critiques of Asian American Images* and *The Outlaw Bible of American Poetry*.

Jason Sanford Brown is an engineer living in Tucson, Arizona, and the editor of *Roadrunner Haiku Journal* online.

Victory Lee Schouten is on the Washington Poets Association board, and is Chair of WPA's annual Burning Word poetry festival. Her poetry books are, *Wolf Love*, (2000 Great Path Publishing), and *Snapshots from a Moving Life*, (2005 Walter Shoe Press).

Gerald Schwartz, author of *Only Others Are* (released by Legible Books, 2003), lives in West Irondequoit, New York.

Alan Semerdjian is a writer/teacher/musician/artist. His writing has been published in numerous print and online journals. His digital home for work is www.alanarts.com.

A graduate with Ph.D. in French literature from the University of Paris, **Fatima Shahnaz** is the author of twelve books, seven of which are poetry, four books of articles and speeches, and one novel, *Golconda* (Booklinks Corp). Shahnaz is the president of the India peace organization and is working in India on drought, agricultural plight of farmers, starvation and other issues afflicting poor countries.

Ravi Shankar is Poet-in-Residence at Central Connecticut State University and founding editor of the international online journal for the arts http://www.drunkenboat.com. His book *Instrumentality* was published by Cherry Grove in 2004. He currently reviews poetry for the *Contemporary Poetry Review*.

Naomi Shihab Nye is a Palestinian-American poet living in San Antonio, Texas. Her recent books include *19 Varieties of Gazelle*; *Poems of the Middle East*, a National Book Award finalist, and *Habibi*, a novel for teens. She has three books forthcoming in 2005, *A Maze Me*, *Going Going*, and *You and Yours*.

Aleda Shirley is the author of two collections of poetry: *Long Distance* (Miami University Press, 1996) and *Chinese Architecture* (University of Georgia Press, 1986), which won the Poetry Society of America's First Book Award.

Sparrow enjoys long conversations, on any subject. He neither smokes nor drinks. Sparrow is a gossip columnist for *The Phoenicia Times*, a newspaper in the Catskill Mountains.

Selene Steese has been writing all her life. "It seems," she says, "as though I tumbled out of the womb with a pen in my hand." Selene is a prolific poet, with several hundred poems to her credit. "Writing is what gets me out of bed in the morning," she says. "I live for words."

Carl Stilwell is 70 years and lives in Pasadena, CA. He has been published in *Pearl*, *Verve* and *Pemmican* and also *An Eye for an Eye Makes the World Blind: An Anthology of Poems on 911*.

Mary Strong Jackson is a poet and a medical social worker. She lives in the Panhandle of Nebraska. Her poetry has appeared in *Times of Sorrow, Times of Grace: Writing by Women of the Great Plains/High Plains*; Papier-Mache Press in its anthology *At Our Core Women Writing About Power*; (Foothills Publishing/Springfed Press Chapbook Series), and *Pudding House Magazine*.

Barbara Tomaine was born and raised in Scranton, PA. She is a graduate of Keystone College and Mansfield Univ. with Bachelor's in English. Tomaine received Paralegal Certification from Ogontz/Penn State. Tomaine's prose and poetry has been published in *Mansfield's Falcon*.

Born in New Orleans, **Katherine Tracy** received a BA in English and also in French from Southeastern Louisiana University where she is currently in her final semester for the MA in English. She is the assistant editor for Louisiana Literature Press and the editor for *L'Intrigue Webzine*—www.lintrigue.org.

George Wallace is editor and publisher of *Poetrybay*, author of 11 chapbooks of poetry, and co-host of the poetry radio show *Poetrybrook USA*. A frequent contributor to *Newsday* as well as a number of weekly community newspapers on Long Island, in 2003 he was named the first poet laureate for Suffolk County.

Jim Warner is currently working on his Master of Arts in Creative Writing at Wilkes University where he is a Graduate Assistant. His book of poetry, *Paper Hearts Made Easy*, is forthcoming by Foothills Publishing.

Former psychology researcher, writer, editor, lecturer, **Patricia Wellingham-Jones** is widely published in journals, anthologies and online. She won the 2003 Reuben Rose International Poetry Prize (Israel) and is a three-time Pushcart Prize nominee.

Teresa White has been published widely online and in print. She was nominated in 1999 for a Pushcart Prize by the Melic Review. She is the author of a book of poems, *In What Furnace?*

Scott Wiggerman has one poetry book, *Vegetables and Other Relationships* (Plain View Press, 2000), and has been published in the *Paterson Literary Review*, *Illya's Honey*, *Borderlands: Texas Poetry Review*, *Midwest Poetry Review*, *Spillway*, *New Texas*, and *Black Buzzard Review*. In addition, he is one of the founding editors of *Dos Gatos Press*, which will take over publication of the Texas Poetry Calendar this year.

Tad Wojnicki is the author of *Lying With Love* and *Under the Steinbeck Oak*, and he lives in Carmel, CA, leading poetry pow-wows on the beach and teaching www.writelikealover.com workshops.

Shin Yu Pai is the author of *Unnecessary Roughness* (xPressed, 2005),

Equivalence (La Alameda Press, 2003), and *Ten Thousand Miles of Mountains and Rivers* (Third Ear Books, 1998). *Nutritional Feed* (Tupelo Press) and *Works on Paper* (Convivio Bookworks) are forthcoming.